Farming on the Sea

By Kellie Peters

Story, photo illustrations, and maps by Kellie Peters
Island view & seal photographs courtesy of Jennifer Nolan

Oyster diagram illustration by Sam Peters

ISBN: 1482057565
ISBN-13: 9781482057560
Library of Congress Control Number: 2013901710
CreateSpace Independent Publishing Platform
North Charleston, South Carolina

ACKNOWLEDGMENTS

Many thanks to Meghan Laslocky, Kristen Lindquist, Stephanie Marshall, Steve Seidell, and Liza Walsh for their kind support and editing wisdom; to my many creative teaching colleagues and my students for loads of inspiration; to Tonie Simmons, owner of Muscongus Bay Aquaculture, for the access to her hatchery; to my professor, Dr. Carol Story, for that first children's literature assignment all those many years ago; and to my family for all their hard work on our oyster farm.

CONTENTS

My name is Sam. Today my sister, Kate, and I are going to work with our dad on our family's farm. Dad's going to teach us about farming, but it won't involve soil or plants. We will wear protective gloves, life jackets, and waterproof boots.

Can you guess where we will be farming and what we grow?

My family grows American oysters in the Damariscotta River, a tidal *estuary* (a body of water that is a combination of both salt and fresh water) of midcoast Maine, at our farm, Norumbega Oyster.

An oyster is a *mollusk* (also called a *bivalve*). That is a type of shellfish that has a soft body tucked inside two shells that are connected by a hinge. Oysters live on the bottom of the ocean. They *siphon* seawater into their bodies (through the opening between their shells) and filter out algae (or *phytoplankton*) for food. They can filter up to four gallons of water every hour. There are many types of true oysters: American, European Flat, Olympia, and Pacific.

Sam's sketch of the inside of our American oysters:

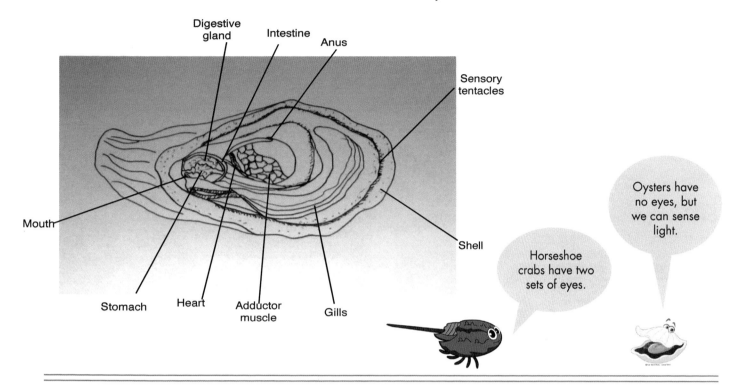

Did you know?

- One serving of oysters has three times more iron than a serving of beef, chicken, or even brussels sprouts, and more iron than a cup of cooked spinach.
- Two-thirds of marine *aquaculture* is mollusks such as mussels, clams, and oysters (the other third is shrimp, salmon, and other finfish).
- When oysters are in their larval stage they have a velum that they use for movement and feeding. As they change into shelled animals, they no longer need the velum.
- The farming of aquatic species (*aquaculture*) has been practiced for over two thousand years.
- Sea stars, certain snails, humans, birds, worms, and crabs are some of the many predators of oysters.
- Oysters are harvested from sea farms and also from the ocean where they grow in the wild.

Before heading to the sea farm, we are going to a shellfish hatchery to see where Dad gets his baby oysters each year. At the hatchery, the mature (adult) oysters, *broodstock,* are kept in tubs of ocean water at a cool temperature until they are ready to create millions of baby oysters called *seed* (the word used to describe very tiny, young oysters).

Large tubes of algae are grown and fed to the broodstock and the baby oyster seed. This room is kept very warm and bright so the algae can grow. Algae need a specific temperature water and the sun's light (or manmade) to grow.

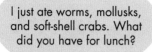

I just ate worms, mollusks, and soft-shell crabs. What did you have for lunch?

Algae is my favorite!

Muscongus Bay Aquaculture Hatchery

We need to find out how many extremely small oyster seed are in a drop of the water. I use a microscope in the hatchery's lab to count the oyster larvae in a drop of water. There are hundreds!

The baby oysters are so tiny that *millions* of them fit in one sandwich-size package. The baby oyster seed are still far too small to set on the ocean floor to grow on their own. The millimeter-size seed might drift away in the tide current, so in the spring the oyster farmers either set them in plastic mesh trays, lay them in small mesh bags, or put them in screened containers that float in a dock called an *upweller*. The oysters will grow in these safe containers until they are big enough to live in larger, floating bags for the rest of the summer.

How many tiny oyster larvae fit in a drop of water?

Hundreds!

It's time to head out on the water with my dad and sister to care for all the growing oysters on our sea farm. As I carefully steer the boat out of the harbor, Dad teaches me about the natural obstacles to avoid, such as rocks and shallow areas. As we travel on the water to the farm, we can smell the salt in the air, hear gulls calling, and see a family of seals basking on the rocks.

Out on the coastal waters in the Northeast there are ospreys, ducks, terns, gulls, seals, finfish, and an occasional whale. In other coastal areas of the United States there are similar birds and animals, and, depending on where you are, you might also see walruses, sea otters, manatees, sharks, porpoises, and stingrays.

There are so many creatures living above and below the water near our sea farm. My sister carefully holds a horseshoe crab by its shell. She never holds it by its tail or legs, so she doesn't bother or harm it in any way, and she places it back in the water very carefully. Horseshoe crabs are called "living fossils" because of how little they've changed in almost five hundred million years.

Today we raise bags of oysters that are six months old out of the water, remove the seaweed, and check to see if they are growing well. After we clean each bag, we lower it back into the water. At this age they are approximately one inch long. The young oysters will grow in bags all summer. In the fall we will set them on the bottom of the sea, where they will spend two more years eating and growing until they are ready to be harvested.

There is a lot of work to be done on the farm every day.

I grow in a mix of fresh and salt water.

Me too, but I need salt water to live.

Today the weather is warm and calm, but there are times when it can be dangerous. If it rains too much, the oysters will filter the ocean water that has temporarily become polluted by waste drained off the nearby lands. After the weather clears, the ocean water becomes clean again and the oysters return to being perfectly healthy. Every day, Dad checks the weather forecast before going to work. Dad also has to look at a tide chart to know how deep the water will be on our farm. When the tide is in, the water on some sections of our farm can be thirty feet deep and when the tide is out, some parts have no water at all.

On land, a farmer *harvests* the crops by pulling them up from the soil or picking them from plants. Dad *SCUBA* dives to the bottom of the sea to pick up all the three-year-old oysters we are going to sell. He designed a special net for gathering oysters from the ocean floor.

When Dad goes under water to harvest oysters, he wears a wet suit to keep him warm. When the water is very cold he wears a dry suit that keeps the icy-cold water from touching his skin, except for his hands and face. Sometimes he SCUBA dives late into the fall or early winter, when the water is so cold it makes his hands and face numb. He also wears a mask over his eyes, so he can see; a buoyancy compensator (which is a vest, that fills with or releases air) to help him float or sink; and a regulator to give him air to breathe from the tanks he wears on his back.

I breathe oxygen from the water through my gills.

Me, too. and I can seal up my shell and stay alive for a while if I'm out of the water.

As Dad picks up the oysters he has to be sure they are alive and healthy. Do you know how to tell if an oyster is no longer alive?

If the shell is open, the oyster is no longer alive and is not safe to eat. After we gather the harvest, Dad shows me how to choose the best oysters to sell.

My scientific name is *Chelicerate* I'm related to spiders and scorpions.

My scientific name is *Ostreidea*, I'm in the "true oyster" family.

The harvested oysters stay in submerged bins filled with ocean water. They are carefully sorted, counted, and cared for.

On our sea farm we grow American oysters, but they aren't the only things grown in aquaculture farms. In oceans, lakes, and rivers all over the world people also farm cod, salmon, trout, mussels, scallops, clams, halibut, seaweed, worms, fish eggs, abalone, red drum, shrimp, cobia, sea bass, tilapia, carp, flounder, red snapper, snook, sturgeon, kampachi, moi, and many more finfish, shellfish, and sea vegetables.

With our oysters on the way to restaurants and seafood shops, we moor our boat and head home for the day.

Being an oyster farmer is a great way to work on the water while enjoying the nature that is all around us.

GLOSSARY

Aquaculture—*to grow and harvest ocean plants or animals on a farm in fresh or salt water.*

Bivalves—*shellfish with two shells.*

Broodstock—*mature oysters that are used for spawning.*

Cultch—*crushed shell and other hard debris on which an oyster attaches itself to stay put and grow.*

Estuary—*salt-water ocean environment that is affected by tides and fed fresh water from a stream or river.*

Harvest—*to gather and collect.*

Mollusk—*shellfish with a hard shell and a soft body. All mollusks are invertebrates (with no internal skeleton).*

Phytoplankton—*microscopic organisms, made up mostly of algae, that drift in the sea or fresh water.*

SCUBA—*Self-Contained Underwater-Breathing Apparatus.*

Siphon—*to pull in or expel liquid.*

Upweller—*a floating dock with circulating water and storage bins for raising shellfish*

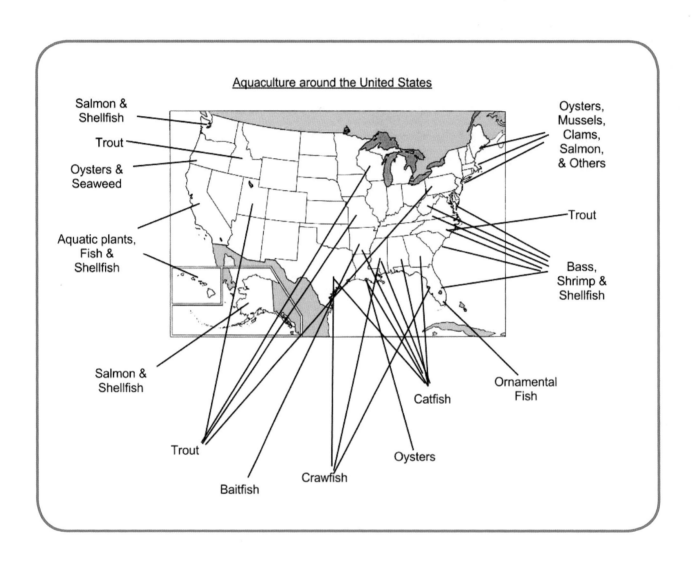

Aquaculture around the United States

Salmon & Shellfish

Trout

Oysters & Seaweed

Aquatic plants, Fish & Shellfish

Salmon & Shellfish

Trout

Baitfish

Crawfish

Oysters

Catfish

Ornamental Fish

Oysters, Mussels, Clams, Salmon, & Others

Trout

Bass, Shrimp & Shellfish

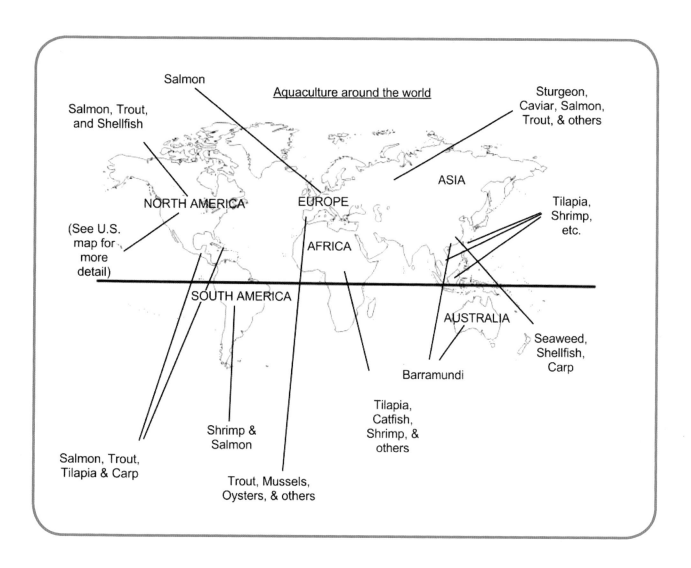

Aquaculture around the world

Salmon

Salmon, Trout, and Shellfish

Sturgeon, Caviar, Salmon, Trout, & others

ASIA

NORTH AMERICA

EUROPE

(See U.S. map for more detail)

Tilapia, Shrimp, etc.

AFRICA

SOUTH AMERICA

AUSTRALIA

Seaweed, Shellfish, Carp

Barramundi

Salmon, Trout, Tilapia & Carp

Shrimp & Salmon

Tilapia, Catfish, Shrimp, & others

Trout, Mussels, Oysters, & others

APPLICABLE SCIENCE STANDARDS

How do the structures of organisms enable life's functions?
External parts of animals and plants help them survive, grow, and meet their needs.
Oysters produce byssus cement that they use to attach themselves to a cultch or resting point on which they plan to stay and grow. Oysters have an organ called a velum that they use for movement and feeding.

What is the process for developing potential design solutions?
Humans can design solutions to problems just as animals overcome natural challenges using their external parts to meet their own needs.
Our harvesters have designed, created, and tested a bag to help collect oysters during harvesting.

How do organisms grow and develop?
Life cycles of plants and animals have similar features and predictable patterns.
Oysters have very specific characteristics at different stages of their growth. The velum is a temporary organ.

How do organisms obtain and use the matter and energy they need to live and grow?
Animal needs include food, water, air, shelter, and favorable temperatures; plant needs include light and water The plants, animals, and other surroundings make up a system in which the parts depend on each other. The algae fed to baby oyster seed is grown in tanks that provide food and light, so the algae continues to grow. Oyster feed on algae and phytoplankton. Oyster farms rely on ocean water and light to grow oysters.

What are the relationships among science, engineering, and technology?
People encounter questions about the natural world every day. There are many types of tools produced by engineering that can be used in science to help answer these questions through observation or measurement. The hatchery, where our seed comes from, uses microscopes as tools to observe and measure the size and quantity of oyster larvae in the water column.

How do natural hazards affect individuals and societies?
Some kinds of severe weather are more likely than others in a given region. Weather scientists forecast severe weather so that communities can prepare for and respond to these events.
Sea farmers rely on the weather for safe growing and harvesting.

HERE ARE SOME QUESTIONS TO THINK ABOUT AND INVESTIGATE

- What are some of the many practical uses for empty oyster shells?
- What is an oyster midden and how can archeologists learn about history by looking at one? Hint: read about the Whaleback Shell Midden and the Glidden Shell Midden in Damariscotta, Maine.
- How old can oysters live to be?
- How can one determine the age of an oyster? (Hint: think about rings on a tree.)
- How large do oysters grow?
- How do the extreme differences in water temperature around the world affect how fast oysters grow?
- How long can different shellfish live, out of water, and still be safe to eat?
- How much do ocean temperatures change between summer and winter in different parts of the world?

INDEX

SUGGESTED RESOURCES

Herring Gut Learning Center <http://www.herringgut.org/>
Maine Department of Marine Resources <http://www.maine.gov/dmr/index.htm>
National Aquaculture Association <http://thenaa.net>
National Oceanic and Atmospheric Administration <www.noaa.gov>

References

"Aquaculture in the Regions." *NOAA Fisheries Service.* 2008. http://www.nmfs.noaa.gov/
aquaculture/supplemental_pages/in_the_regions.html (accessed August 25, 2012).

"Basic Questions about Aquaculture." *NOAA Office of Aquaculture.* http://www.nmfs.noaa.gov/
aquaculture/faqs/faq_aq_101.html (accessed August 25, 2012).

Gamble, Madi. "All About Aquaculture: Current Status in New England." *Fish Talk.* October 23,
2012. www.TalkingFish.org/did-you-know/all-about-aquaculture-current-status-in-new-england
(accessed January 10, 2013).

"Horseshoe Crab." *Encyclopedia Britannica Online Academic Edition.* Encyclopedia Britannica.
2013. http://britannica.com/EBchecked/topic/272407/horseshoe-crab (accessed January
18, 2013).

"Ostreidae." *Encyclopedia Britannica Online Academic Edition.* Encyclopedia Britannica. 2013.
http://britannica.com/EBchecked/topic/434440/ostreidae (accessed January 18, 2013).

PacAqua (Pacific Aquaculture Caucus) & Fisheries Aquaculture. "State of Aquaculture on the West
Coast." Annual, PacAqua (Pacific Aquaculture Caucus) & Fisheries Aquaculture, 2004.

United States Department of Agriculture. "The Census of Aquaculture." February 7, 2007. (accessed
August 29, 2012).

Walsh, Bryan. "Can the US Close Its Seafood Trade Deficit?" *Science and Space.* July 8, 2011.
www.Science.time.com/2011/07/08/can-the-u-s-close-its- seafood-trade-deficit/ (accessed
January 18, 2012).

Winder, Jessica. "Oyster Velum." *Jessica's Nature Blog.* January 18, 2010. http://natureinfocus.
wordpress.com/2010/01/28/natural-objects-on-which-flat-oysters-settle/ (accessed January
14, 2013).

For complete lists of Science Standards:
Next Generation Science Standards (NGSS) <http://www.nextgenscience.org/>

Made in the USA
Charleston, SC
28 August 2015